NICKELBACK
HERE AND NOW

Produced by
Alfred Music Publishing Co., Inc.
P.O. Box 10003
Van Nuys, CA 91410-0003
alfred.com

Printed in USA.

ISBN-10: 0-7390-8824-6
ISBN-13: 978-0-7390-8824-1

Album Cover Concept: NICKELBACK • Album Art Direction: Gail Marowitz • Album Design: Julian Peploe Studio

CONTENTS

THIS MEANS WAR

Music and Lyrics by
CHAD KROEGER

This Means War - 7 - 1

6

8

Chorus:
w/Rhy. Figs. 2 *(Elec. Gtr. 2)* **& 2A** *(Elec. Gtr. 1), both 2 times*

Who do you think you are?___

Is this what you came for?___

Well, this means war._____

Outro:
w/Rhy. Figs. 3 *(Elec. Gtr. 2),* **3A** *(Elec. Gtr. 1),* **& 3B** *(Elec. Gtr. 3), each 1st 4 meas. only*

Well, this means war.___

w/Rhy. Figs. 3 *(Elec. Gtr. 2),* **3A** *(Elec. Gtr. 1),* **& 3B** *(Elec. Gtr. 3)*

Elec. Gtrs. 2 & 3

Elec. Gtr. 2

BOTTOMS UP

Music and Lyrics by
CHAD KROEGER, MIKE KROEGER
and JOEY MOI

Chorus:

This is what it's all a-bout, no one can slow us down. We ain't gon-na stop un-til the

clock runs out. (Bot - toms up!) Hell can't han-dle all of us, so get your bot-tles up.

Drink-in' ev-'ry drop un-til it all runs out. 'Noth-er round,___ fill 'er up,___ ham-mer down,___

*Tap note w/R.H. index finger, snap off to next note w/R.H. index finger, then slur (pull off) with L.H. finger.
 Hold both left hand notes down for each triplet group when tapping first note in group.

Chorus:

Bass gtr. tacet 8 measures.

w/Rhy. Fig. 2 *(Keybd.) 3 times*

This is what it's all a-bout, no one an slow us down. We ain't gon - na stop un - til they

Rhy. Fig. 2
Keybd.
(arr. for gtr.)

mf

Elec. Gtr. 1

throw us all out. Hell can't han - dle all of us, so get your bot - tles up.

WHEN WE STAND TOGETHER

Music and Lyrics by
CHAD KROEGER, Mike KROEGER,
RYAN PEAKE and JOEY MOI

Moderately slow ♩ = 96

*Recording sounds a half step higher than written.

Verse:

1. One more de-pend-ing on a prayer,___ and we all look a-way.
2. They tell us ev-'ry-thing's all right,___ and we just go a-long.

Peo-ple pre-tend-ing ev-'ry-where,___ it's just an-oth-er day.
How can we fall___ a-sleep at night,___ when some-thing's clear-ly wrong.

There's bul-lets fly-ing through the air,___ and they still car-ry on.
When we could feed___ a starv-ing world___ with what we throw a-way.

We watch it hap-pen o-ver there,___ and then just turn it off.
But all we serve___ are emp-ty words___ that al-ways taste the same.

When We Stand Together - 3 - 1

𝄋 *Chorus:*

Am Fsus2 G Am Fsus2

13 *Resume rhy. fig. simile*

We must stand to-geth - er

(Hey,__ yeah,__ yeah, hey, yeah.) (Hey,__ yeah,__ yeah, hey, yeah.)

G Am Fsus2 G

16

There's no giv-ing_____ in. Hand in hand for-ev -

(Hey,__ yeah,__ yeah, hey, yeah.)

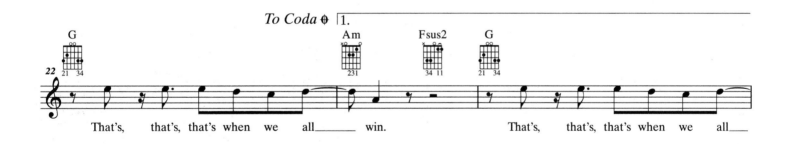

Am Fsus2 G Am Fsus2

19

- er That's when we all_____ win.

(Hey,__ yeah,__ yeah, hey, yeah.) (Hey,__ yeah,__ yeah, hey, yeah.)

To Coda ⊕ │1.

G Am Fsus2 G

22

That's, that's, that's when we all_____ win. That's, that's, that's when we all__

║2.

Am Fsus2 G Am Fsus2 G

25

__ win. __ win. That's, that's, that's when we all__

(Hey,__ yeah,__ yeah, hey, yeah.)

Bridge:

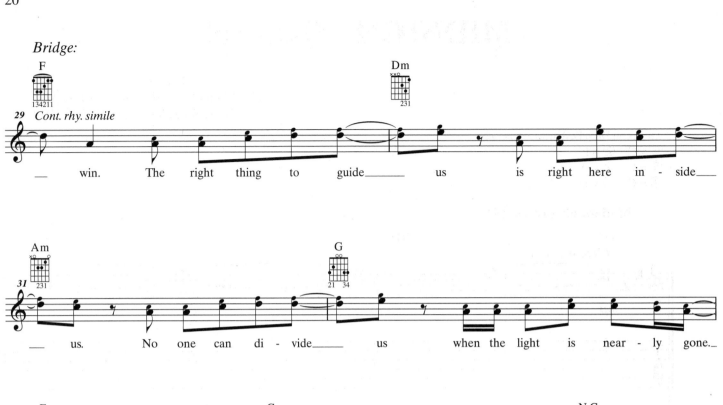

win. The right thing to guide_____ us is right here in - side_____

us. No one can di - vide_____ us when the light is near - ly gone._____

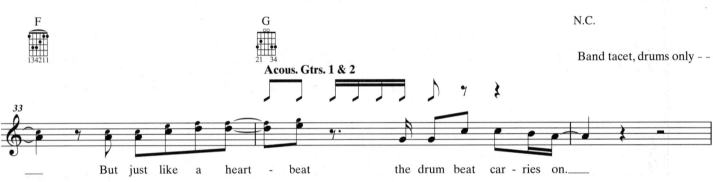

N.C.

Band tacet, drums only − −

Acous. Gtrs. 1 & 2

_____ But just like a heart - beat the drum beat car - ries on._____

D.S. 𝄋 al Coda

And the drum beat car - ries on._____ Just like a heart - beat.

⊕ *Coda*

_____ win. That's, that's, that's when we all_____ win.

MIDNIGHT QUEEN

Music and Lyrics by
CHAD KROEGER, MIKE KROEGER,
RYAN PEAKE and JOEY MOI

*All gtrs. in Drop D, down 1 whole step:
⑥ = C ③ = F
⑤ = G ② = A
④ = C ① = D

Moderately fast ♩ = 152

Intro:

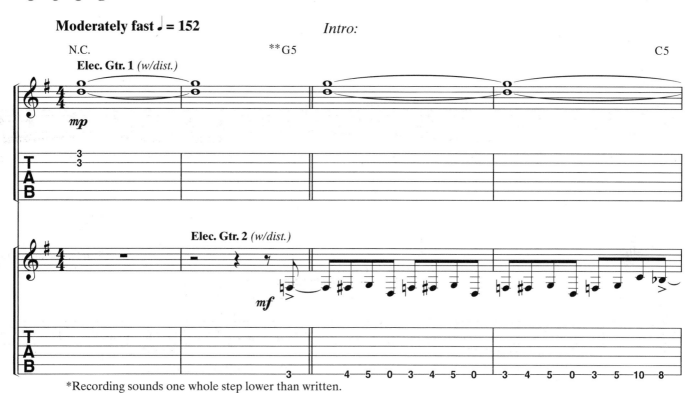

*Recording sounds one whole step lower than written.

**Chords are implied for four measures.

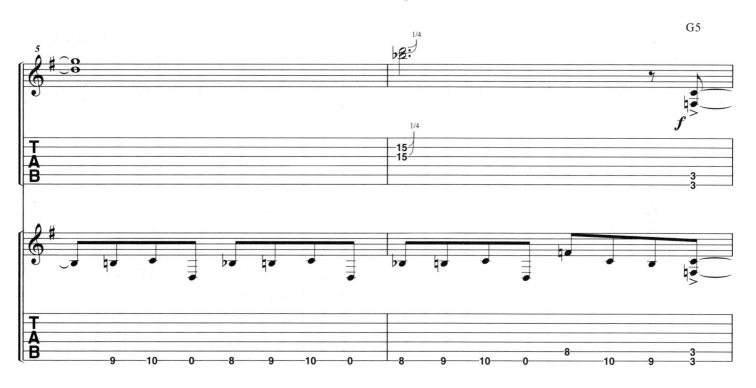

% *Chorus:*

*Chord implied by bass gtr.

Guitar Solo:
Elec. Gtr. 3 tacet

GOTTA GET ME SOME

Music and Lyrics by
CHAD KROEGER and JOEY MOI

*All gtrs. in Drop D, down 2 whole steps:
⑥ = B♭   ③ = E♭
⑤ = F   ② = G
④ = B♭   ① = C

Moderately slow ♩ = 82

Intro:

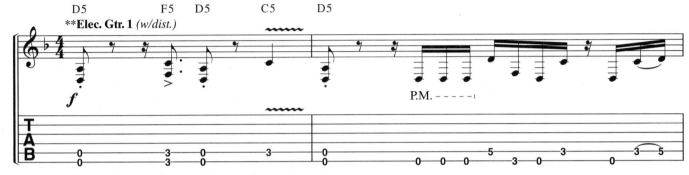

*Recording sounds two whole steps lower than written.
**Elec. Gtr. 1 is a composite arrangement.

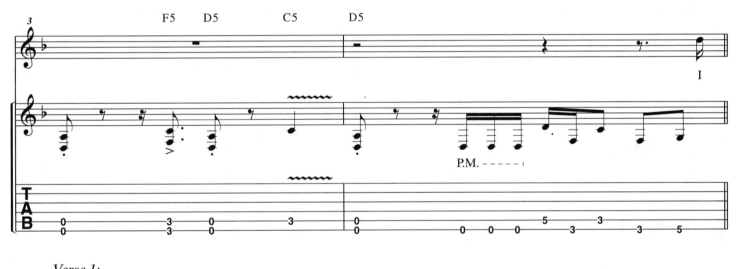

Verse 1:

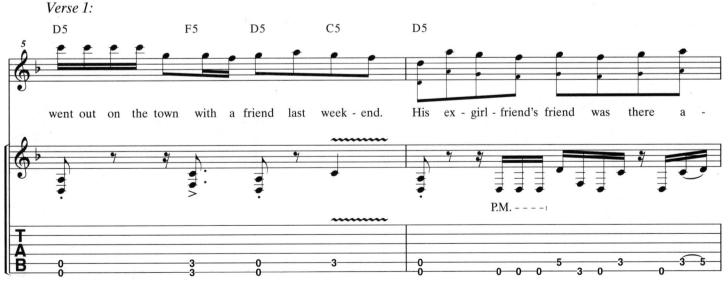

went out on the town with a friend last week-end. His ex-girl-friend's friend was there a-

Lyrics:
She's a scene from a Bay-watch re-run. Hot-ter than a bar-rel on a squeeze ma-chine gun.

Guitar Solo:

She smokes a lit-tle

✸ *Coda*

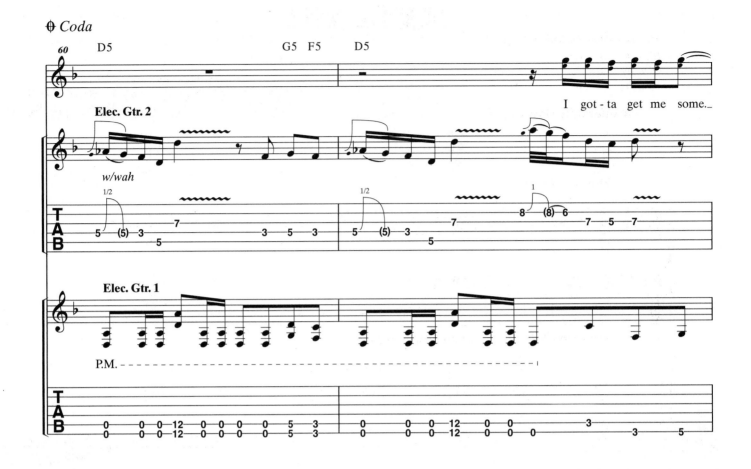

I got - ta get me some.___

Elec. Gtr. 2

w/wah

Elec. Gtr. 1

P.M.

Elec. Gtrs. 1 & 2 tacet

N.C.

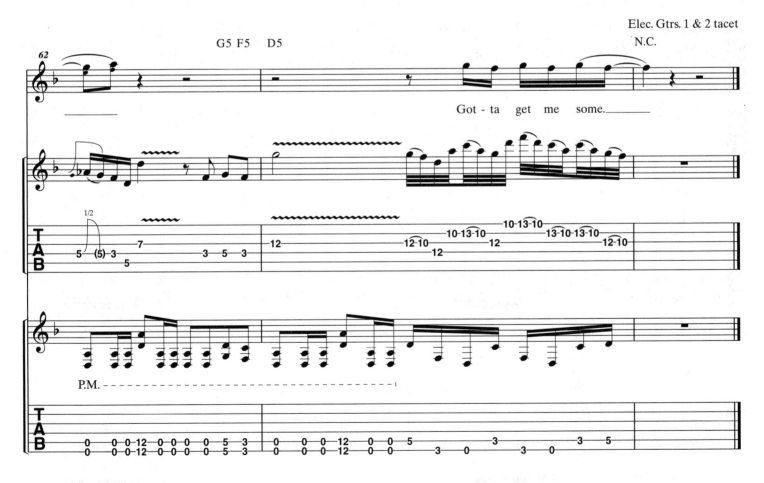

Got - ta get me some._____

P.M.

LULLABY

*All gtrs. in Drop D, down 1/2 step:
⑥ = D♭   ③ = G♭
⑤ = A♭   ②= B♭
④ = D♭   ①= E♭

Music and Lyrics by
CHAD KROEGER, CRAIG WISEMAN,
RODNEY CLAWSON and CHRIS TOMPKINS

Moderately slow ♩ = 74

*Recording sounds a half step lower than written.

Intro:

Elec. Gtr. 1 (w/light dist.)

1. Well, I know the feel-

Verse:
Elec. Gtr. 1 tacet

-ing_____ of find-ing your-self_____ stuck out on the ledge.__ And there ain't no heal-
(2.)__ you_____ out of the dark-ness and in-to the light.__ 'Cause I have faith__

-ing_____ from cut-ting your-self_____ with the jag-ged edge.__ I'm tell-ing you__
__ in you__ that you're gon-na make__ it through an-oth-er night.__ Stop think-ing a-bout

To Coda ⊕ | 1.

D5   F5   C5   G5

23

- la - by.___   Your ver - y own lul - la - by.___   2. Please let me take_

| 2.   *Bridge:*   Band tacet

C5   G5   C

Piano *(arr. for gtr.)*

25

- la - bye._   Well, ev - 'ry - bod - y's hit___ the bot - tom.

Am7   F(9)

27

And ev - 'ry - bod - y's been_ for - got - ten.___   When ev - 'ry - bod - y's tired_ of be - ing a - lone.___

C   Am7

29

Yeah, ev - 'ry - bod - y's been_ a - ban - doned.   And left a lit - tle emp - ty hand - ed.___

D.S. % al Coda

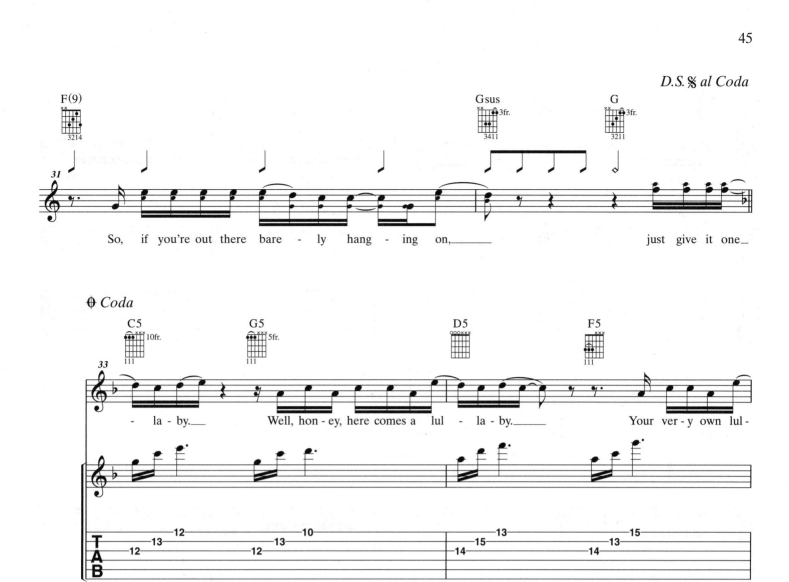

So, if you're out there bare - ly hang - ing on,_____ just give it one_

⊕ *Coda*

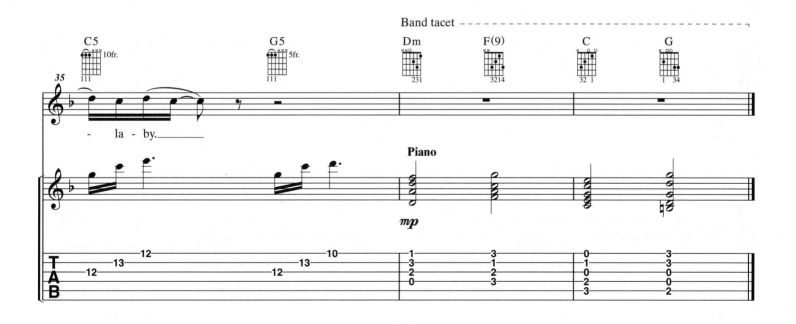

- la - by._ Well, hon - ey, here comes a lul - la - by._ Your ver - y own lul -

- la - by._

KISS IT GOODBYE

Music and Lyrics by
CHAD KROEGER, MIKE KROEGER
and JOEY MOI

*All gtrs. in Drop D, down 1 1/2 steps:
⑥ = B ③ = E
⑤ = F♯ ② = G♯
④ = B ① = C♯

Moderately ♩ = 112

Fade in

N.C.

Synth.

Elec. Gtr. 1 *(w/dist.)*

p

*Recording sounds one and one half steps lower than written.

f

Intro:

A5 G5 A5 C5 G5 A5 G5 A5 D5 G5

(Kiss it good - bye,___

w/slight P.M. - - - - - - - - - -

Pre-chorus:

Chorus:

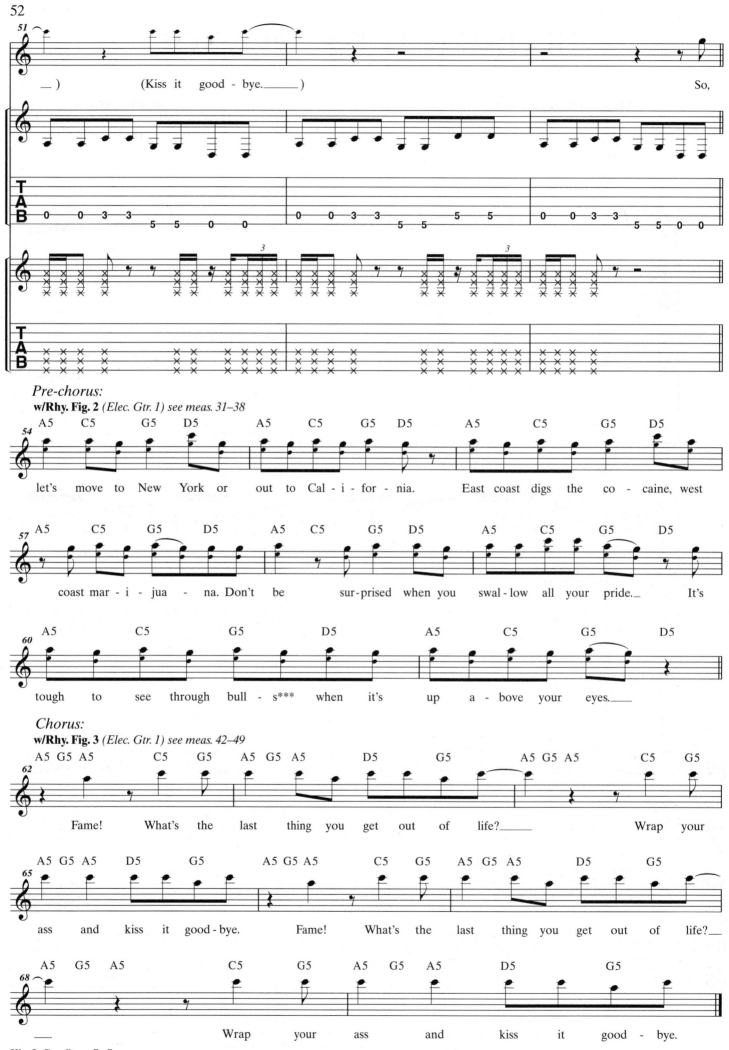

Pre-chorus:
w/Rhy. Fig. 2 *(Elec. Gtr. 1) see meas. 31–38*

Chorus:
w/Rhy. Fig. 3 *(Elec. Gtr. 1) see meas. 42–49*

TRYING NOT TO LOVE YOU

Moderately slow ♩ = 86

Intro:

Music and Lyrics by
CHAD KROEGER, RYAN PEAKE
and BRAD WARREN

56

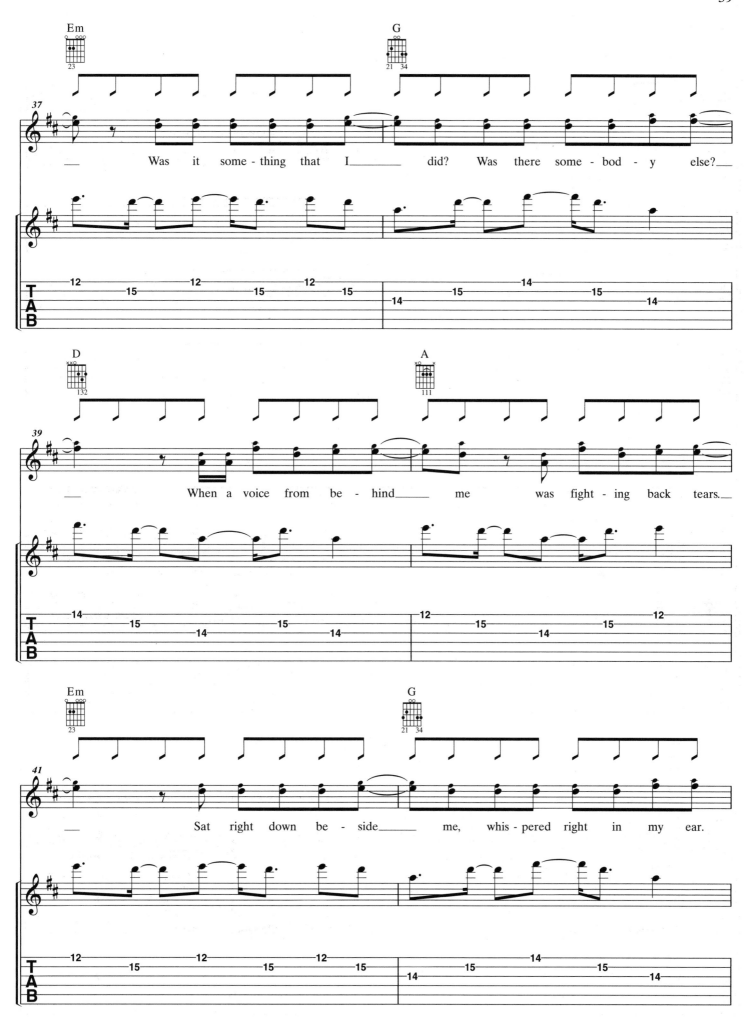

Chorus:
Band tacet 4 meas.

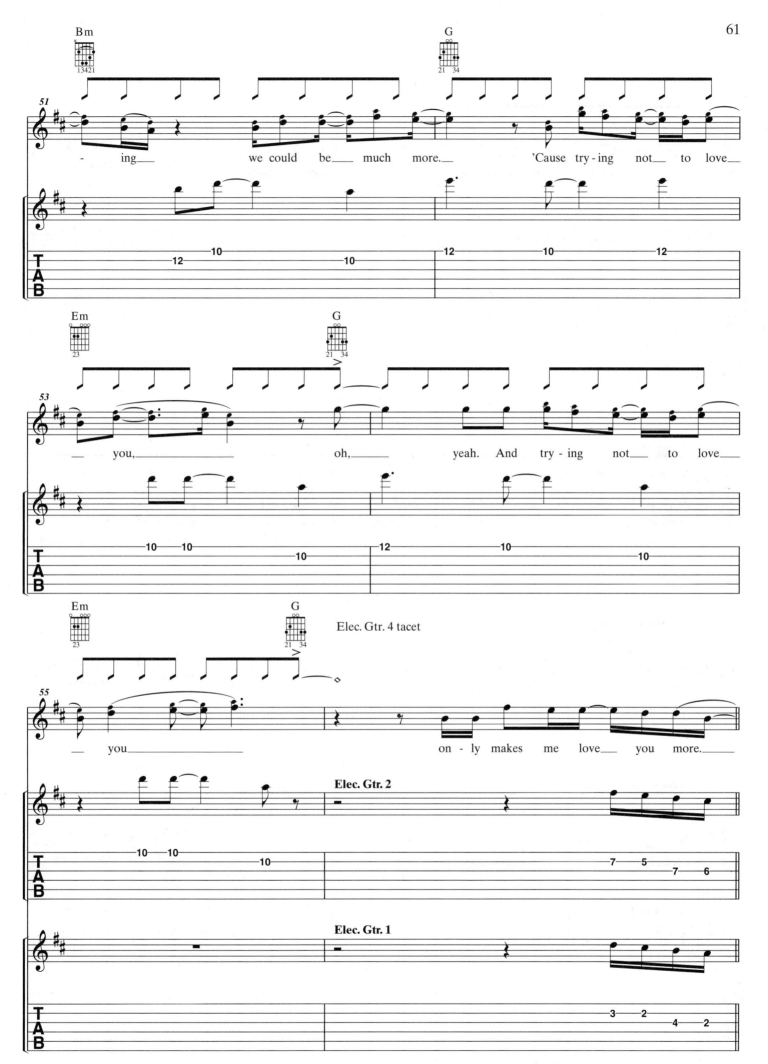

*This last measure is actually a digital delay
repeating beat 4 of the previous measure.

HOLDING ON TO HEAVEN

Music and Lyrics by
CHAD KROEGER and MIKE KROEGER

Moderately slow ♩ = 82

*Chords are implied, shown for reference.

And if for - ev - er nev - er comes,__ then I... And if for - ev - er nev - er comes,__ then I... And if for-

Elec. Gtr. 1 (w/dist. & tremolo)

ev - er nev - er comes,__ then I... I'll hold__ on and hold__ on.

Verse:

Elec. Gtr. 2 (clean-tone w/chorus)

1. I keep lis - t'ning to my chest
2. And if I can write a sym - pho - ny,

Elec. Gtr. 3 (clean-tone)

P.M.

Holding on to Heaven - 9 - 1

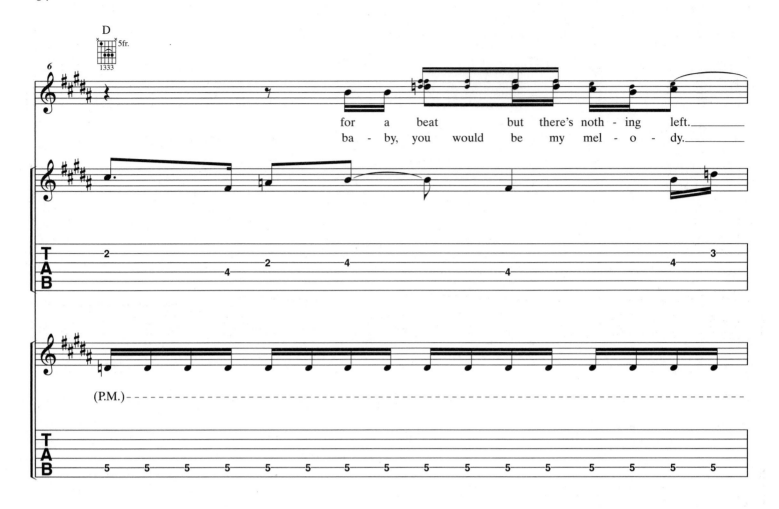

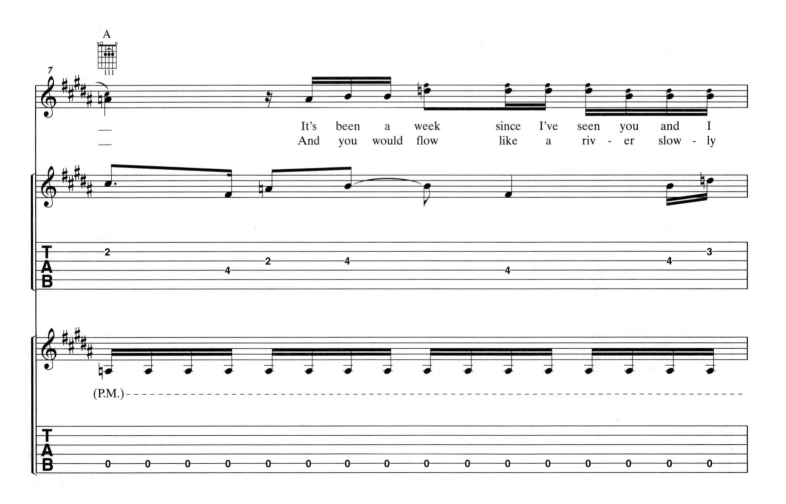

66

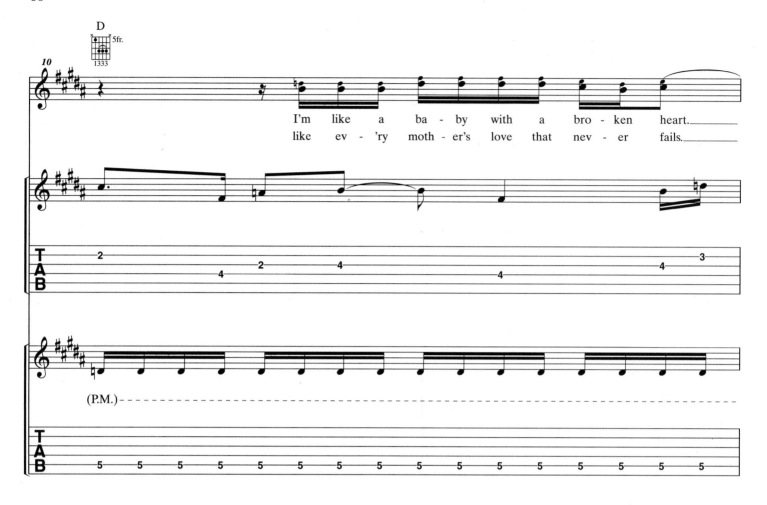

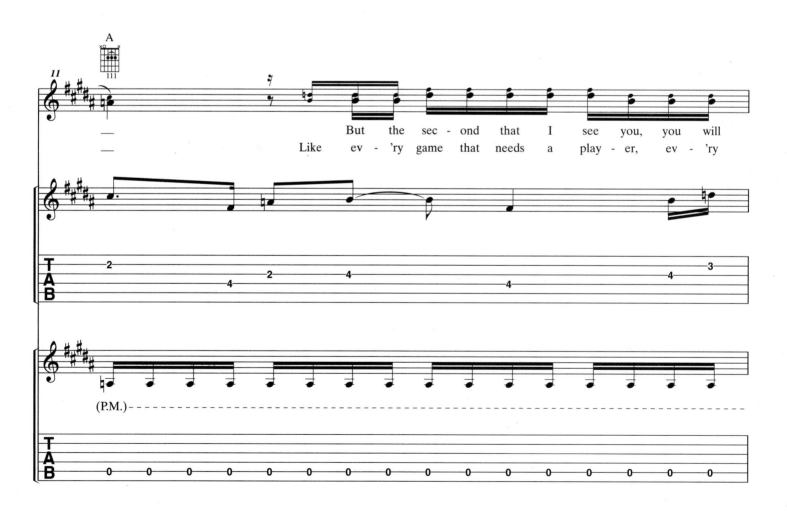

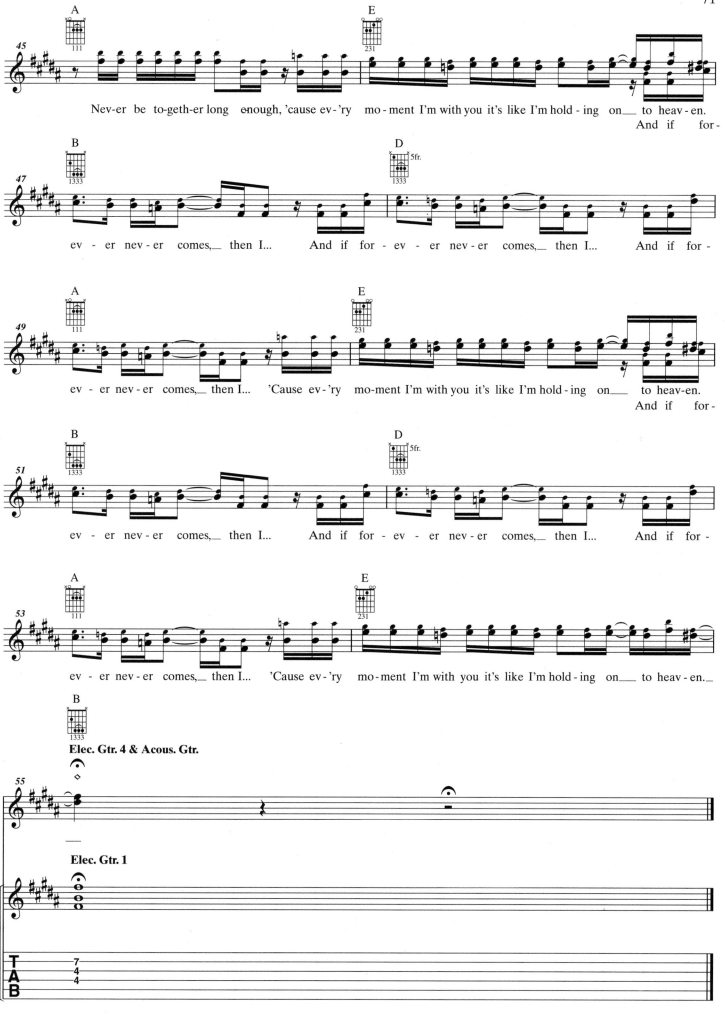

A
E
ev - er nev - er comes, then I... I'll hold on and hold on.
2.
E
B
mo - ment I'm with you it's like I'm hold - ing on to heav - en. (Heav - en, heav - en, heav - en.)
Bridge:
G
A
And I'm will - ing to wait just to see you an - oth - er day.
Will - ing to wait.
E
What I'm wait - ing for, we'll wash this pain a - way.
Wash, this, a...
G
A
And it's nev - er too late. And if for -
Nev - er to late.

EVERYTHING I WANNA DO

Music and Lyrics by
CHAD KROEGER

*All gtrs. in Drop D, down 1 whole step:
⑥ = C ③ = F
⑤ = G ② = A
④ = C ① = D

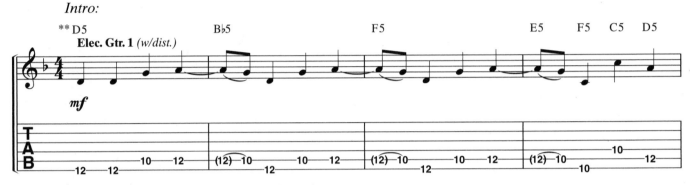

Moderately fast ♩ = 160

w/half-time feel

Intro:

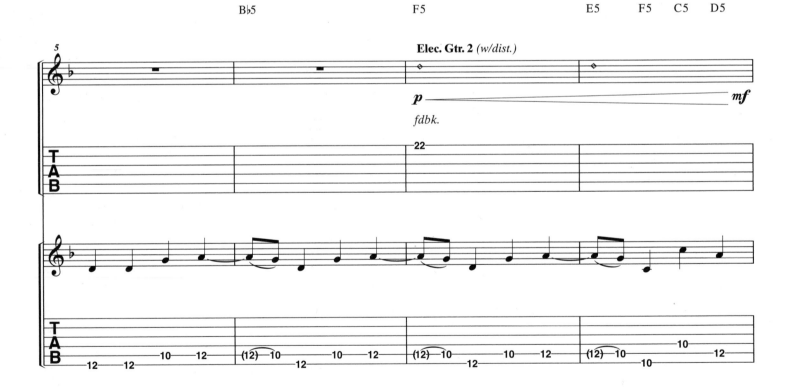

*Recording sounds one whole step lower than written.
**Chords are implied.

Everything I Wanna Do - 8 - 1

Verse 1:
Elec. Gtrs. 1, 2, & 3 tacet

She's___ got a dirt - y mouth,___ it tastes so clean___ with ev - 'ry

*Chords implied by bass gtr.

taste of me.___ You know that ev - 'ry sin - gle thing___ she does, she

does for me___ be - cause it's what I'm dream - ing of.

Chorus:

end half-time feel
Guitar Solo:

w/slight P.M. throughout

resume half-time feel

Pre-chorus:

w/Fill 1 *(Elec. Gtr. 5) see meas. 36*

N.C.

(You and me sit-ting in a tree, F * * * I N G.)

grad. bend

Elec. Gtr. 4

Chorus:

w/Rhy. Figs. 2 *(Elec. Gtr. 3)* **& 2A** *(Elec. Gtr. 2), both 4 times*

She'll do an-y naugh-ty thing I want. My ba-by, she's up for an-y-thing I wan-na do.

She's a giv-er and it gets her off. My ba-by, she's in-to ev-'ry-thing I wan-na do. If

DON'T EVER LET IT END

Music and Lyrics by
CHAD KROEGER

Don't Ever Let It End - 7 - 1

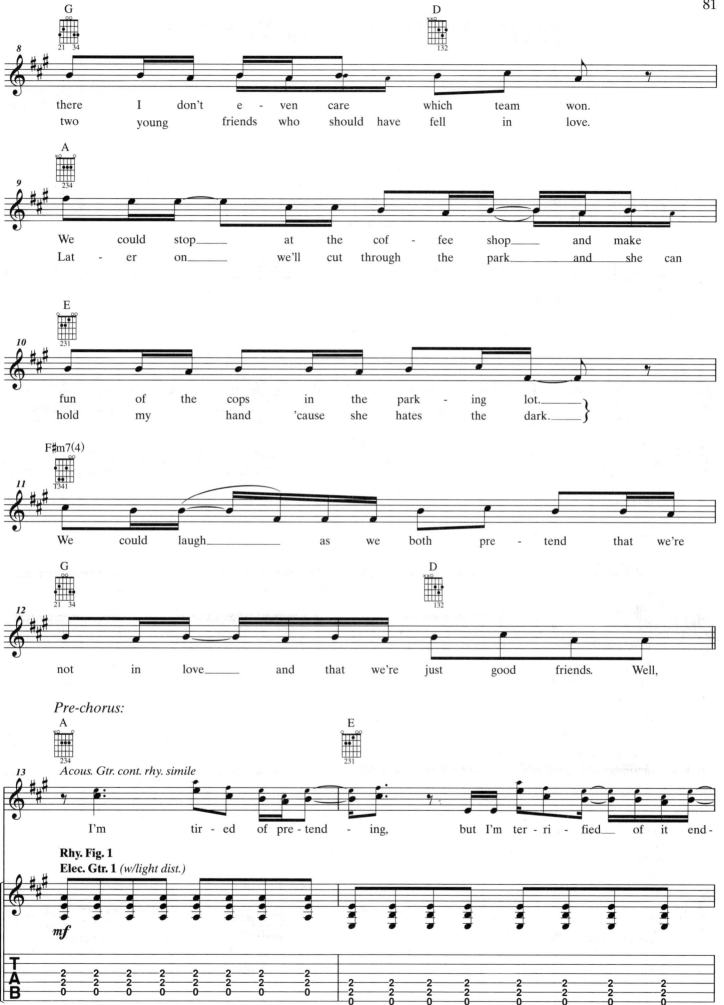

Verse 3:
Band tacet 8 meas.

Acous. Gtr.

Sun - day night,___ just her and I___ sit - ting side by side in the full moon - light.___ I

pulled her close___ just to hold her tight and the both of us___ could tell it just felt right. She

looked at me___ in the sweet - est way___ like she could tell what the hell I was a - bout to say.___ Must have

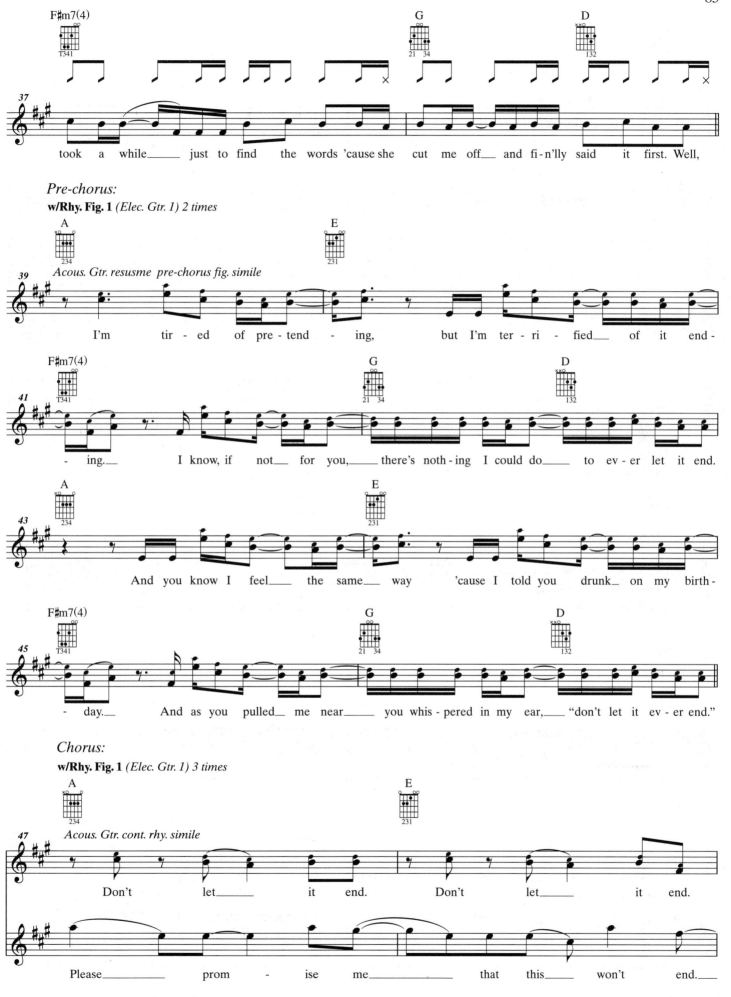

TABLATURE EXPLANATION

TAB illustrates the six strings of the guitar.
Notes and chords are indicated by the placement of fret numbers on each string.

GUITAR TAB GLOSSARY

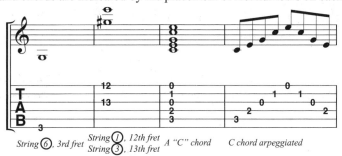

String ⑥, 3rd fret String ①, 12th fret A "C" chord C chord arpeggiated
String ③, 13th fret

BENDING NOTES

Half Step:
Play the note and bend string one half step (one fret).

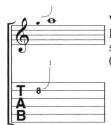

Whole Step:
Play the note and bend string one whole step (two frets).

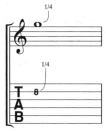

Slight Bend/ Quarter-Tone Bend:
Play the note and bend string sharp.

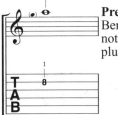

Prebend (Ghost Bend):
Bend to the specified note before the string is plucked.

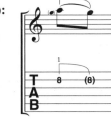

Prebend and Release:
Play the already-bent string, then immediately drop it down to the fretted note.

Unison Bends:
Play both notes and immediately bend the lower note to the same pitch as the higher note.

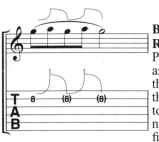

Bend and Release:
Play the note and bend to the next pitch, then release to the original note. Only the first note is attacked.

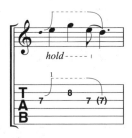

Bends Involving More Than One String:
Play the note and bend the string while playing an additional note on another string. Upon release, relieve the pressure from the additional note allowing the original note to sound alone.

Bends Involving Stationary Notes:
Play both notes and immediately bend the lower note up to pitch. Return as indicated.

ARTICULATIONS

Hammer On:
Play the lower note, then "hammer" your finger to the higher note. Only the first note is plucked.

Pull Off:
Play the higher note with your first finger already in position on the lower note. Pull your finger off the first note with a strong downward motion that plucks the string—sounding the lower note.

Legato Slide:
Play the first note and, keeping pressure applied on the string, slide up to the second note. The diagonal line shows that it is a slide and not a hammer-on or a pull-off.

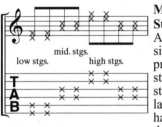

Muted Strings:
A percussive sound is produced by striking the strings while laying the fret hand across them.

Palm Mute:
The notes are muted (muffled) by placing the palm of the pick hand lightly on the strings, just in front of the bridge.

HARMONICS

Natural Harmonic:
A finger of the fret hand lightly touches the string at the note indicated in the TAB and is plucked by the pick producing a bell-like sound called a harmonic.

RHYTHM SLASHES

Strum Marks/ Rhythm Slashes:
Strum with the indicated rhythm pattern. Strum marks can be located above the staff or within the staff.

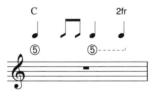

Single Notes with Rhythm Slashes:
Sometimes single notes are incorporated into a strum pattern. The circled number below is the string and the fret number is above.

Artificial Harmonic:
Fret the note at the first TAB number, lightly touch the string at the fret indicated in parens (usually 12 frets higher than the fretted note), then pluck the string with an available finger or your pick.

TREMOLO BAR

Specified Interval:
The pitch of a note or chord is lowered to the specified interval and then return as indicated. The action of the tremolo bar is graphically represented by the peaks and valleys of the diagram.

Unspecified Interval:
The pitch of a note or chord is lowered, usually very dramatically, until the pitch of the string becomes indeterminate.

PICK DIRECTION

Downstrokes and Upstrokes:
The downstroke is indicated with this symbol (⊓) and the upstroke is indicated with this (V).